The Science of Living Things

How do Animals Move?

Niki Walker & Bobbie Kalman

Crabtree Publishing Company

www.Crabtreebooks.com

The Science of Living Things Series
A Bobbie Kalman Book

For my grandparents, Nick and Marie
with love

Editor-in-Chief
Bobbie Kalman

Writing Team
Niki Walker
Bobbie Kalman

Managing Editor
Lynda Hale

Project Editor
John Crossingham

Editors
Heather Levigne
Hannelore Sotzek
Kate Calder

Copy Editor
Heather Fitzpatrick

Computer Design
Lynda Hale

Photo Researcher
Kate Calder

Consultant
K. Diane Eaton, Hon. B.Sc., B.A., Brock University

Photographs
Animals Animals/Stephen Dalton: page 30 (top)
Robert McCaw: page 30 (bottom)
Tom Stack & Associates: Jeff Foott: title page, page 6; Kitchin and Hurst:
    page 27; Joe McDonald: pages 18, 22, 29; Doug Sokell: page 9;
    Dave Watts: page 23; David & Tess Young: page 19
Merlin D. Tuttle, Bat Conservation International: page 28 (bottom)
Other images by Digital Stock and Eyewire, Inc.

Illustrations
Barbara Bedell: pages 5, 6 (bottom), 7, 9, 10, 11, 12, 13 (left), 15 (dolphin),
    17, 21 (top, bottom right), 23, 24, 25, 26, 29 (bottom)
Anne Giffard: page 19
Jeannette McNaughton-Julich: page 15 (flukes)
Bonna Rouse: pages 6 (top), 13 (right), 16, 21 (left), 29 (top)

Digital Prepress
Embassy Graphics

Printer
Worzalla Publishing Company

Crabtree Publishing Company

PMB 16A	612 Welland Ave.	73 Lime Walk
350 Fifth Ave.,	St. Catharines,	Headington,
Suite 3308	Ontario,	Oxford
New York, NY	Canada	OX3 7AD
10118	L2M 5V6	United Kingdom

Cataloging in Publication Data
Walker, Niki
    How do animals move?

(The science of living things)
Includes index.

ISBN 0-86505-981-0 (library bound) ISBN 0-86505-958-6 (pbk.)
This book introduces various methods of animal locomotion, discussing
gaits, flight, aquatic movement, and more unconventional variations.

1. Animal locomotion—Juvenile literature. [1. Animal locomotion.] I. Kalman,
Bobbie. II Title. III. Series: Kalman, Bobbie. Science of living things.

QP301.W276 2000   j573.7/9 21   LC 99-085746
                                                                           CIP

Contents

How do animals move?

Most animals can move from place to place. They move to find food and shelter, escape danger, and hunt. Animals need to move in order to survive.

From here to there

Animals move in many ways. Some propel themselves through water; some crawl along the ground; and others soar high in the sky. How an animal moves depends on the structure of its body and where the animal lives. Most animals with wings fly, those with fins and **flukes** swim, and animals with legs crawl, walk, hop, or run.

(above) Birds fly by pushing down on the air with their wings.

(top) On land, animals move by pushing against the ground.

Hunters and the hunted

Many **predators**, or hunters, use speed to catch their **prey**, or the animals they hunt. Animals that are hunted often use confusing movements to escape their predators. They dodge, weave, and sprint so their attacker will not be able to guess where they will move next.

Non-movers

Some sea creatures such as anemones and corals move only while they are very young. They swim in search of a good place to live and anchor themselves in one spot. Once they are anchored, they do not move again. Instead, they catch their food as it floats by.

This springbok runs, leaps, and makes zigzag turns to avoid predators.

(above) Sea fans and other types of coral are anchored in one spot.

(left) Feather-duster worms cannot move from place to place, but they can extend their tentacles to trap food.

The bare bones of movement

Animals have many shapes and sizes. Their body is supported by a **skeleton** and **muscles**, which allow them to move in different ways. There are three types of skeletons: **hydrostatic** skeletons, **exoskeletons**, and **endoskeletons**.

earthworm

Hydrostatic skeletons

Animals with hydrostatic skeletons do not have any bones. They are called **invertebrates** because they have no backbone. Their body is a tube of muscle filled with liquid, which is their skeleton. The animals move by squeezing their muscles and forcing their skeleton to change shape.

Exoskeletons

Insects and crabs are invertebrates that have an exoskeleton. An exoskeleton is outside the body. It surrounds an animal's body like armor. It supports and protects the soft parts inside. Animals with exoskeletons can move and bend only where they have **joints**, which move in one direction only. Muscles underneath the skeleton **contract**, or shorten, to bend the joint back and forth.

fiddler crab

joint

exoskeleton — muscle

exoskeleton joint

Endoskeletons

Birds, fish, mammals, amphibians, and reptiles are **vertebrates**—they have a backbone. All vertebrates have an endoskeleton, which is inside the body and is made up of bones and **cartilage**. It gives the body its shape and protects the most important organs such as the heart and brain. Animals with endoskeletons are more flexible than those with exoskeletons. Many of their joints can move their body parts in different directions. A pair of muscles attached to each bone moves it back and forth.

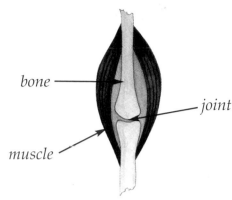

bone

joint

muscle

In order to move the bones of an endoskeleton joint, one muscle contracts while the other stretches.

Hip joints determine the position of an animal's legs. Mammals and birds have their legs underneath their body. A reptile's legs come out of the sides of its body.

Ball-and-socket *joints, such as the shoulder and hip, allow movement in several directions.*

Hinge *joints, such as the knee and elbow, bend in one direction only.*

Pivot *joints, such as the ankle and wrist, can rotate and bend in any direction.*

African elephant

Squeezing by

Snails produce a shell, which is their home. They pull their house with them wherever they go.

Animals such as earthworms, snails, and slugs do not have bones or legs. They have hydrostatic skeletons and move from place to place by crawling on or through the ground. To crawl, they contract and stretch their muscles.

Slimy trails

Snails and slugs move slowly, using a single muscle called a **foot** on the bottom of their body. They move by contracting, or squeezing, parts of their foot, raising the parts forward, and then placing them down. This motion pulls the animal's body along the ground.

To make traveling easier, snails and slugs put down a layer of **mucus**, or slime. The mucus is slippery when touched lightly, so the raised, contracted parts of the foot slide forward easily. When the mucus is pressed, however, it becomes firm and gives the other parts of the foot a better grip.

Thick and thin

An earthworm's body is made up of **segments**, or sections. Each segment is a packet of fluid surrounded by muscle. To crawl, the worm squeezes some of its segments so that they become long and thin and stretch forward. It makes the other segments short and fat and pushes them against the ground for grip.

Even when moving on its trail of mucus, a slug's foot appears motionless from the side.

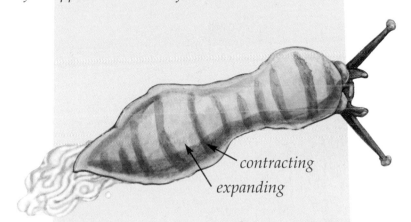

contracting

expanding

This underside view of a slug shows the contracted and relaxed parts of the foot in motion. The contracted parts, shown here as darker lines, are lifted slightly off the surface and slide forward with a wavelike motion.

When the stretched segments reach as far as they can, the worm shortens them to pull the rest of its body forward. (See the earthworm illustration on page 6.)

The jet set

(above) Squid are strong swimmers. Some can eject themselves thirteen feet (4 m) above water and land on the decks of boats!

Some **aquatic** invertebrates are **jet propelled**—they use jets of water to shoot themselves from place to place. Octopuses, squid, and scallops all use jet propulsion. They move in a series of stops and starts as they take in water and shoot it out.

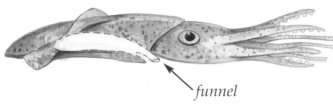

funnel

Think of the squid's air cavity as a balloon, and the funnel as the balloon's opening. If you release a full balloon, air rushes out of the opening and sends the balloon flying.

Point and shoot

Squids take in water through a slit on their belly. They shoot it out through a narrow tube called a **funnel**. A squid can point its funnel in different directions to send itself forward, backward, up, down, left, or right.

Slamming shut

A scallop has a protective shell that is **hinged**, or joined, in the middle. A scallop does not move around much. When an enemy gets close, however, it jets away by slamming together the two halves of its shell. As it closes its shell, the water inside rushes out through two small openings near the back of the animal. This rush of water shoots the scallop away from danger. It is similar to the swoosh of air you feel when you slam a door.

(top) When using jet propulsion, an octopus keeps its tentacles trailing straight behind, allowing water to pass easily around its body.

(above) Starfish hunt scallops. Scallops can escape a hungry starfish, but they cannot use jet propulsion for very long because they tire easily.

Fishy moves

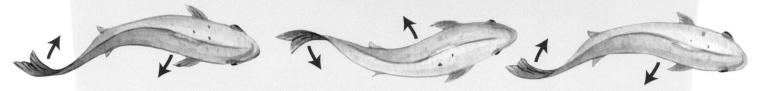

Many people think that fish push themselves through water with their fins, but fish use their fins mainly for steering. Almost all fish travel by making wavelike movements with their body. A fish moves its body from side to side and swishes its tail back and forth. This motion pushes the water around the fish backward, in order to propel the fish forward.

*(below) Unlike other fish, a stingray does not have a large tail for pushing water backward. Instead, it moves by sending wave motions from front to back along its large **pectoral** fins.*

Dorsal and **caudal** *fins keep the fish from rolling over. The fish also uses these fins to turn left or right.*

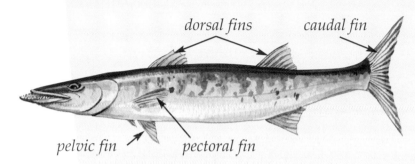

dorsal fins   caudal fin

pelvic fin   pectoral fin

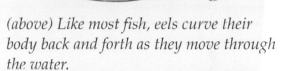

Pectoral and **pelvic** *fins are found in pairs on either side of the fish. The fish uses them to steer up and down.*

(above) Like most fish, eels curve their body back and forth as they move through the water.

(below) Many fish that live in coral reefs have fins that allow them to steer among tight spaces in the coral. Some fish can **hover**, *or remain in one spot.*

Water wings

Some aquatic animals seem to move more like birds than fish! Their body parts are similar in shape to the wings of birds. These strong, winglike parts are called **hydrofoils**. Hydrofoils move up and down instead of from side to side. As the hydrofoil moves, it pushes the water backward around the animal. This motion also keeps the animal from sinking. Penguins, sea turtles, sea lions, and whales have hydrofoils.

Penguins are birds, but they cannot fly. Instead, they are excellent swimmers. They flap their wings underwater to move themselves forward quickly. They steer with their feet and tail. As they swim, they look as though they are flying!

Penguins are covered with feathers that are smaller and more scalelike than those of other birds. These feathers make their body more streamlined so the birds can move easily through water.

What a fluke!

Dolphins, shown right, and other whales have a tail that is shaped to help push them through water. Their tail is made up of two hydrofoils called flukes. These mammals move their flukes up and down in the water to push themselves forward and keep from sinking. Some whales move only their tail as they swim, whereas others bend their whole body up and down while moving their tail.

flukes

(top) A shark's pectoral fins act as hydrofoils but they do not move up and down. The fins stay still. As the shark swims through water, the fins help keep it afloat.

Strokes

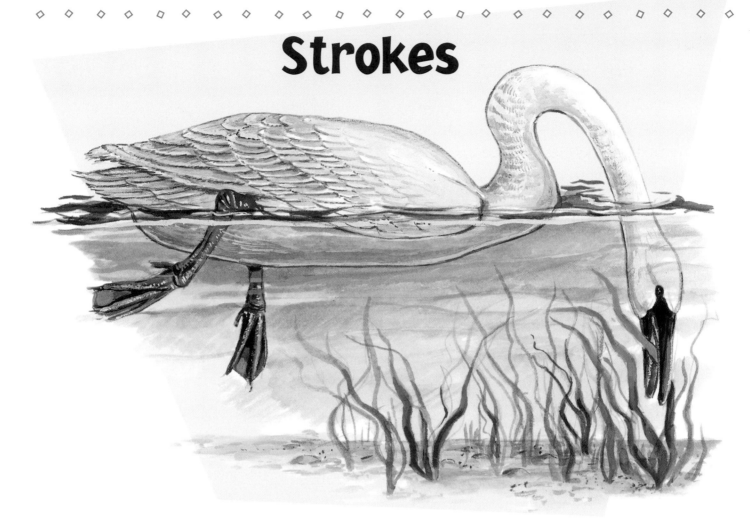

In the water, many animals travel by using movements that are similar to those of land animals. As they use their legs to **row** or **paddle**, they often appear to be walking or running through the water. Animals that row move their legs at the same time, in the same way people move oars in a rowboat. Animals that paddle move their legs one at a time, like the motion of people paddling a canoe.

Most birds that swim have webbed feet. To paddle, they spread the webbing on one foot to create a larger "paddle" and then push it backward through the water. As they push with the one foot, the other foot moves forward. They tightly press the toes of the forward-moving foot together, allowing the foot to slip smoothly through the water.

Swans can easily feed on water plants while paddling through shallow water.

Hairy paddles

Water beetles have hairs called **bristles** on their legs that are used for rowing. When they push against the water, the beetles spread the hairs to make their legs wider. These wider legs allow the insects to push more water, so they can move farther and faster with each stroke. When pulling their legs forward, the beetles tuck the hairs close to their legs.

Snap shot

Much of the time, crustaceans such as shrimp and crayfish walk along coral reefs or on the ocean floor. When frightened, however, these invertebrates make a fast escape. They spread the hard plates of their fanlike tail and snap their tail quickly against their underside. This action sends a rush of water away from their body and propels the animal backward.

Smooth moves

Snakes are vertebrates that do not have limbs. Instead, they use their long body to crawl. To move, large snakes such as pythons use a **rectilinear motion**. They lift sections of their belly and pull themselves ahead. Most snakes, however, use their muscles to pull their skeleton into "S" shapes as they move.

The black mamba is the world's fastest snake. It travels at about six miles (10 km) per hour, but it can move as fast as twelve miles (19 km) per hour.

Doing the wave

To travel, a snake bends itself into curves and then pushes the curves backward along its body. The front and back of each curve presses against a surface so the rest of the snake can move forward. Small, rough scales on its belly help the snake grip the ground. Snakes cannot move very fast on a smooth surface because their belly has little to grip.

*(left) On loose sand, snakes **sidewind**. They coil their body and then fling themselves sideways.*

*(below) In **serpentine motion**, snakes push against rocks and other objects to move themselves forward.*

*In tight spaces, snakes use a **concertina motion**—they pull up their body and then extend it.*

Snakelike movements

In water a crocodile or an alligator, shown left, uses the same "S"-shaped movement a snake does. Crocodiles and alligators tuck their legs against their body and then bend from side to side. This motion allows these reptiles to move quickly and easily through water.

Legs on land

Most land animals, including people, use their legs to move from place to place. Some have two legs, some have four, and others have hundreds of legs. Land animals sometimes move one leg at a time, but often they move two or more at a time. An animal must be able to keep its balance as it lifts its legs and brings them forward.

(above) When humans run, both their feet are off the ground between steps.

(top) Four-legged animals bend their back up and down as they run. This motion helps them swing their legs faster and use less energy as a result.

One foot in front of the other

A **gait** is the pattern of an animal's steps. **Bipeds**, or two-legged animals, have two normal gaits: walking and running. **Quadrupeds**, or four-legged animals, use up to eight gaits including walking, **trotting**, **cantering**, and **galloping**.

When horses walk, they move a front leg and the opposite hind leg together. A trot is similar to a walk but is slightly faster. When cantering, three of the horse's feet are off the ground at once. During a gallop, however, none of its feet touch the ground between steps.

The mudskipper, shown above, and climbing perch are fish that can leave the water for a short time to walk on land. They use their front fins as legs to pull themselves along the ground.

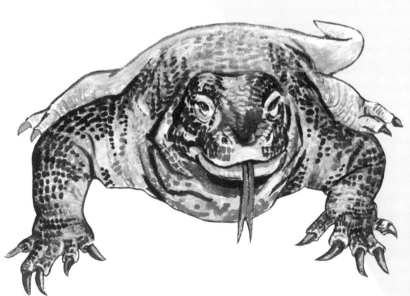

Reptiles such as lizards, alligators, and crocodiles have legs that stick out from the sides of their body. They move with a **sprawling gait**. These animals bend their body from side to side to take each step.

Millipedes have hundreds of legs. They move their legs in order from front to back so they will not trip on them.

Leaps and bounds

Animals such as frogs, kangaroos, rabbits, and grasshoppers find it easier to leap than walk from place to place. Hopping also helps these animals escape enemies. They can take off quickly from a still position, and they can fool their enemies by unexpectedly changing direction as they bounce.

Frogs land on their front legs. They must hop in single bounds, which means they stop between each leap.

Snap to it

Animals that jump have powerful hind legs that are much longer than their front ones. When resting, the animals stand on bent legs. To leap, they quickly snap their legs straight. They push off the ground with great force and send themselves high into the air.

furcula

Fleas leap 200 times their own height! This springtail, or snow flea, has an organ under its rear called a furcula that helps it spring up.

Kangaroos leap when they need to move in a hurry. They land on their hind legs, so they do not need to stop between hops. When moving slowly, kangaroos shuffle on all four legs. They use their long tail as a fifth "leg" for balance.

Climbing

Many animals scurry up tree trunks to escape enemies or find food. Some live in the treetops. Many of these animals are not only expert climbers, but they also have found interesting ways to get from tree to tree.

Going up...

To climb a tree trunk, an animal grips it with all four legs. It holds onto the trunk and pulls itself up with its front paws while pushing against the tree with its hind paws. Most animals have claws to help them grip the bark. Tree frogs and some lizards have sticky foot pads. They can climb trees and slippery surfaces such as walls.

Tree climbers, such as this raccoon, get a great view of the world below. They can watch for enemies or search for food.

Animals, such as bush babies, often leap from tree to tree instead of climbing down the trunks. They push off with their hind legs, stretch out their front legs, and grab the next tree with their claws.

As a gibbon begins to swing, its legs hang. When it stretches for the branch, it bends its legs close to its body. Stretching and bending its legs helps a gibbon gain speed.

Swingers

The arms of most primates are longer than their legs. Long arms are helpful in climbing. Gibbons use **brachiation** to move among trees. They hang from a branch with one hand and then swing forward to grab a second branch with the other hand.

Coming down...

Many animals can climb up trees but not all can climb down again. Animals that are able to climb down trees, such as squirrels, have hind feet that turn around so their claws can dig into the bark.

Cats are great at climbing trees, but they often have trouble getting down! They cannot turn their hind feet backward, so their claws are unable to grip the tree.

Gliding

Animals such as flying squirrels, flying frogs, and flying lizards have developed body parts suited for traveling from one tree to another. They have flaps of skin that they spread out and use for gliding. Although these animals are called "fliers," they do not actually fly. They cannot move their flaps up and down the way birds move their wings.

(above) A flying squirrel steers with its tail and limbs when gliding.

flying lizard

In the air without wings

Flying squirrels have a flap of skin called a **patagium** on each side of their body. It is located between their front and hind legs. To glide, these animals climb to a high branch and spread their limbs as they jump. Their skin is pulled tight like a kite, allowing them to coast to a lower branch or the next tree. A flying lizard also has flaps of skin along each side of its body, but these flaps are attached to its rib bones. The lizard extends its rib bones to tighten its flaps for gliding. It bends the bones back when it is not using the flaps.

*The flaps of skin between the long toes of flying frogs are called **webs**. When the frog leaps from a tree, it spreads its toes. The webs act as parachutes to slow down the animal's fall.*

Flapping flight

(above) Bats have wings made of skin that is stretched over their long fingers, but bats are not able to glide as birds can. They must flap their wings constantly to stay in the air.

Birds, bats, and some insects can move in a way no other animals can—they fly. All of these animals have wings that flap up and down to lift them off the ground and move them forward through air. Flying has many benefits. It allows animals to escape from enemies on the ground, to swoop and catch prey, and to find food and shelter in places that other animals cannot reach.

In a flap

When birds flap their wings, they push down on the air and create **lift** and **thrust**. Lift raises and keeps the bird in the air. Thrust moves the bird forward. Feathers produce thrust by pushing against the air.

Soaring

Flapping is tiring work, so birds often rest their wings by gliding and **soaring**. To soar, birds use columns of warm air called **thermals**. This warm air rises above the cool air around it. A bird spreads its wings and allows the thermal to push itself up. When the bird exits the thermal, it glides downward in search of another thermal on which it can soar.

faster air

slower air

A wing's curved shape helps create lift. All air moving above and below the wing must reach the other side of the wing at the same time. Air traveling over the wing has farther to go, so it moves faster. The air underneath is slower. It pushes up the wing and helps support the bird in the air.

(above) Most insects have two pairs of thin, stiff wings. Some flap all four wings together, and others flap each pair separately. Insects flap their wings so quickly that they make a buzzing sound.

(left) Insects are too light to soar or glide without getting blown out of control by the wind. Instead, they must always use flapping flight when they are in the air.

Different moves

Some animals have a different way of getting around. The pictures on this page show a couple of the many unusual moves animals use to get from one place to another.

Water walkers

Some animals, such as the basilisk above, can run on water. The surface of water is like a thin, stretchy skin. As long as an animal does not break the "skin," it can walk on water and will not sink. Most water walkers have long toes or hairs on their legs that help spread out their weight. The animal does not sink because only a small part of its weight touches each point on the water's surface.

*(above) An inchworm travels by **looping**. It has small legs at the front of its body but none at the back. It pulls its back end directly behind its legs and crawls forward until its body is flat. The inchworm then loops its back end forward again.*

How do we move?

People have many ways of moving from place to place. We can walk, run, crawl, climb, swim, and jump, but if we want to fly, we need to do it in a helicopter or airplane! Name all the ways you move your body each day. Which **vehicles** do you use to help you move from place to place quickly? Do you have a favorite way of moving?

(above) We use our arms to climb the monkey bars like a brachiating gibbon. We hold on with one hand and reach forward with the other one.

(above) We may not have fins, flippers, or flukes, but we can still swim. Our feet and hands push the water around our body backward.

(right) We can bend at the knees and then push off the ground with our legs for a giant jump!

Words to know

aquatic Describing a living thing that lives in, on, or near water

cartilage A strong, flexible material found in some parts of the body, such as the nose and ears

endoskeleton A skeleton that is made up of bone, cartilage, or other hard material, and is inside an animal's body

exoskeleton The hard outer shell of certain types of animals

gait The way that an animal moves on foot, such as walking or galloping

hydrofoil A winglike part of an animal's body

hydrostatic skeleton A skeleton that is made up of muscle and liquid instead of bones

joint A part of an animal's body that bends and allows the animal to move

paddle To swim by moving one foot after the other

patagium A thin flap of skin on each side of an animal's body. By spreading its patagia, the animal can float and glide through the air.

thermal A current of warm air that rises upward

Index

3 4 5 6 7 8 9 0   Printed in the U.S.A.   9 8 7 6 5 4 3 2